Travel Snapshots

CARIBBEAN

Text by
Eugenio Bersani
Lucia Giglio

Graphic design
Anna Galliani

Map
Giancarlo Gellona

Contents

1 *Man of War Bay is one of the loveliest places along the shores of Tobago, the small island which, with Trinidad, forms an independent nation, separated from South America by as little as 6 miles.*

2-3 *The scenery offered on the east of Barbados is a mix of stunning beaches and stretches of rocky cliffs swept by winds off the Atlantic. Compared with more tranquil Caribbean shores beauty here has a wilder dimension: breakers crashing on rocks at high tide, winds bending the tall palm trees and a prevailing impression of being in contact with the more authentic side of nature.*

4-5 *Nearly touching in Antigua are a freshwater lake and the ocean. Antigua is famed for its many beaches; though they have never been counted, the local people are convinced there are 365, one for every day of the year.*

6-7 *The intense, warm colors of the Tropics illuminate the splendid bay of Gustavia, capital of Saint-Barthélemy, a small French Caribbean island. Gustavia is gaining popularity as a tourist destination, but it is a retreat for the rich and famous (the Rockefellers own large tracts of land here) rather than a playground for the masses.*

8 *On the eastern tip of Guadeloupe is the Pointe des Chateaux, a stunning rocky promontory stretching out into the aquamarine waters of the Caribbean.*

9 *A beautiful face peers out on a narrow street in Castries, capital of St. Lucia.*

12-13 *With beautiful beaches just feet away from coral reefs, Tobago is a scuba diver's paradise.*

Published in North America by
AAA Publishing
1000 AAA Drive
Heathrow, Florida 32746
www.aaa.com

© 1996 White Star S.r.l.
Via Candido Sassone, 22/24
13100 Vercelli, Italy
www.whitestar.it

ISBN 1-56251-805-4
1 2 3 4 5 6 06 05 04 03 02

Printed in Singapore
Color separations by La Cromografica, Ghemme (Novara), Italy

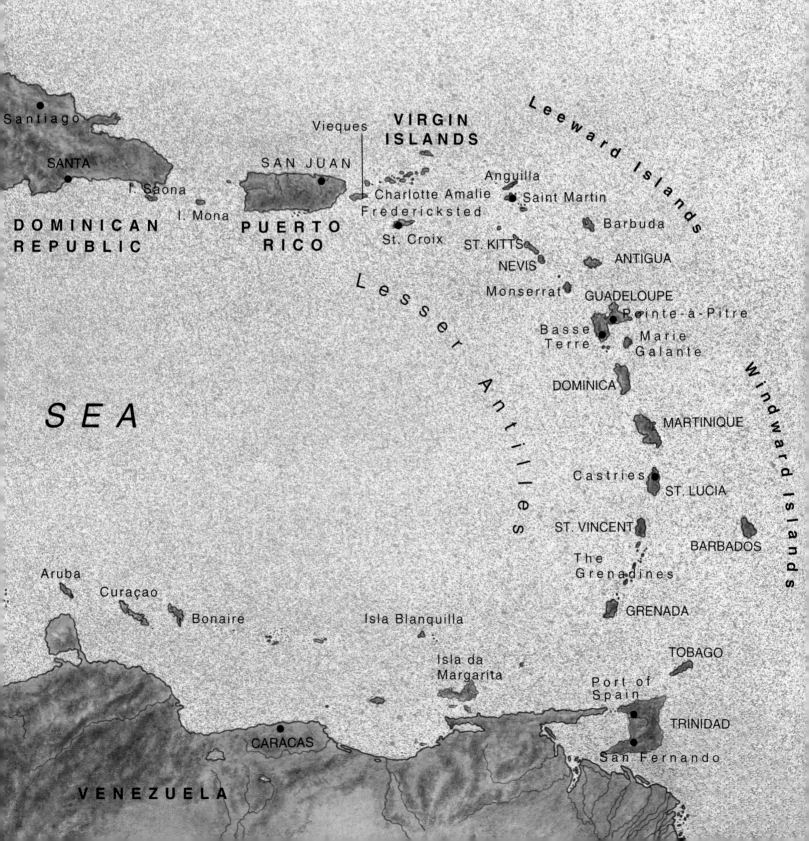

Introduction

Here in the Tropics, lush vegetation fills every inch of space and the sun saps every spark of energy. And yet, however fierce the heat, the Caribbean people abide by their fundamental mission: to enjoy life. On any of the islands, which are scattered between the Tropic of Cancer and the coast of Venezuela, you come across brilliant colors, smiling faces and an irresistible joie de vivre expressed in rhythmic music.

This huge archipelago between North and South America is comprised of a thousand different worlds. No place on earth offers a greater assortment of exotic landscapes: extinct volcanoes, rainforests, green valleys with plantations of sugar cane, rolling hills, mountain ranges and, of course, the ocean. In the last decade or two, it seems that this one remaining paradise of modern times is inexorably destined to become a huge haven for visitors in search of suntans and exotic pleasures. The mythical dimension of these islands and the many legends of romance and adventure that have delighted readers appear to be the epilogue of a past lost forever. But do the glossy pictures in travel brochures really tell the whole story?

Has the Caribbean's links with its fascinating past been severed forever? Delving into their history, we find that every one of these islands has stirring tales to tell. Their "package tour" image is only surface deep. The Antilles are still the legendary lands found by early Renaissance explorers who were searching for the semi-mythical world of Antilia, islands whose existence had been imagined by 15th-century Italian cartographers. Far from being lost, the past of the Caribbean adds a special magic to every aspect of its present. Centuries ago

European civilization and African civilization collided and converged here, and the resulting melting pot is the key to the fascination of today's Caribbean Islands. The Greater Antilles were the scene of fierce battles between Spain, France, England and the Netherlands.

Galleons from Europe sailed homeward from the harbors of Cuba, Hispaniola – now Haiti and the Dominican Republic – Jamaica and Puerto Rico carrying huge cargoes of gold. For many years Europe's seafaring powers struggled to gain control of these rich, fertile lands. It seemed the Lesser Antilles might escape this same cruel fate since, as they had no gold, the Spaniards considered them of no interest. These islands are small, some of them tiny, but still unspoiled. They include the mysterious Windward and Leeward Islands, magical places where buccaneers and pirates once held sway.

Untamed nature and limited space have held in check the excesses of urbanization and the tourist boom, now all too apparent on the bigger islands. Set in the bluest ocean in the world, these places have managed to keep intact their original physiognomy, proud and beautiful. But the disinterest of the great European powers was short-lived.

This time it was the English and French who seized the lovely Windward and Leeward Islands. In the 17th century, the first English colony was established at St. Kitts, and France took possession of Martinique and Guadeloupe. Even the tiniest islands were found to offer fertile terrain for an effortlessly produced new treasure: sugar cane.

Plantations of the profitable crop spread throughout the Caribbean, leading to new conflicts, huge riches for planters and traders, and the importation of many thousands of slaves from Africa. The imposition of European culture had a devastating impact on the "New World."

Today hardly a trace of the native

14 *The "casa de la trova" in Santiago is the most celebrated on the whole island of Cuba: The musicians gathered there every evening offer rousing concerts with their improvised ballads.*

15 top *No product expresses the spirit of Cuban culture better than cigars. Smoking them is more a national passion than a vice.*

15 bottom *During "zafra," the sugar-cane harvest, skilled macheteros are joined by thousands of students and office workers who only occasionally handle a machete.*

Amerindians remains. Every corner of the islands was turned into a piece of Europe, transplanted in the Tropics, to which the importation of slaves from Africa added a additional ethnic component. The world of the sugar plantations survived only at the cost of bitter and bloody confrontation. On one side were the powerful families of estate owners who received land and slaves from the authorities. On the other, masses of exploited, poorly treated Africans. This world collapsed toward the mid-19th century, when its foundations were undermined by the combined forces of the abolition of slavery and competition from sugar beet on international markets. A whole way of life disappeared with it. In Cuba amid the lush greenness of the San Luis Valley stands the Iznaga Tower: this tall belltower is all that remains of the fifty "ingenios de azucar," the sugar factories that brought prosperity to the city of Trinidad.

It is now a symbol of a long-banished past:. From the top of the tower powerful planters kept watch on the slaves toiling among the canes below. The fusion of the disparate cultures of the freed slaves and the descendants of the colonialist settlers resulted in a cultural manifestation, a unique mélange of traditions and influences that differs from island to island. While the Creole culture is strongly influenced by the French charm of Martinique, it is also tinged by the pale colors of houses in the Netherlands Antilles and by the neatness that characterizes the British colonies.

Their scenery may be substantially the same, but the countries of the Caribbean have wide divergencies in culture, language, ethnicity and creativeness. The thirty million inhabitants of the Caribbean Islands are a mix of many races. In the Netherlands Antilles there are descendants of Europeans and Chiqueros Indians who, in these parts, survived longer than elsewhere. The pervasive presence of Europe is most noticeable in the capital towns. The beautiful island of Curaçao is Amsterdam in miniature, as sweet as the liqueur distilled here from fragrant oranges.

The old quarters of its main town, Willemstad, are pure delight, with their ornately decorated Dutch-style gabled houses, painted in the palest shades of pink, blue, green and yellow. Since 1634, when these tiny islands were snatched from the Spaniards, Dutch merchants have used the magnificent natural harbor of Curaçao to increase their trade. Today it is the largest port in the Caribbean and, in terms of volumes of freight handled, one of the foremost trading ports of the world. The island has a sound economy and widespread prosperity – features not common in this part of the world. In its thoroughly democratic society there is real equality of rights, regardless of color or ethnic origin. In Punda, the old trading district of Willemstad, the waterfront still offers an unusual, bustling marketplace – afloat. Boats come all the way from Venezuela to sell fish, fruits and vegetables in a varied row of stalls that draw crowds of shoppers.

Evidence that the Netherlands Antilles are firmly rooted in the modern world is also plentiful. Another snippet of Europe is found in the British possessions: the most northerly of the Leeward Islands were settled peacefully by British colonists in 1627.

After three centuries under British rule, the populations of these islands – called Bajan – think and live much like inhabitants of Britain: their houses have English-style gardens, they make a ritual of afternoon tea and they are great fans of cricket. Admittedly, the rolling hills and green countryside of Barbados are reminiscent of English valleys and the British-sounding names of the island's villages complete the picture.

A visit to English Harbor, a port of Antigua, makes it easy to understand why the bulldog breed fell for the Caribbean's

charms. This beautiful natural harbor, now a haven for luxury yachts, was once the base of the British fleet in the West Indies. Between 1784 and 1787 the officer second-in-command was the future hero of Trafalgar, Admiral Lord Nelson, and the town is practically a shrine to the years he spent here. English Harbor has become a fashionable Caribbean resort, frequented by the rich and famous; its buildings have been restored with British capital, reportedly at the instigation of members of the Royal Family. Old warehouses and waterfront structures have been converted into luxury shops, to ensure that every need of international jetsetters is met in the Caribbean too. Here, as in Curaçao, there is a thriving economy and people live comfortably; unemployment and illiteracy are practically nonexistent. Europe's influence is felt again farther south, in the French Antilles: Martinique and Guadeloupe – French soil set in tropical waters – almost emanate an illusory fragrance of the Côte d'Azur. But nature here has a wilder, almost cruel side. Lording over the islands are still-active volcanoes and the luxuriant vegetation with dazzling colors – hibiscus, orchids, bougainvillea – also stems from the fiery veins beneath the craters. Fort-de-France, administrative capital of Martinique, has much in common with many French coastal towns.

Martinique has also acquired some Western vices: upscale apartment buildings and luxury stores are now commonplace. Fort-de-France itself – birthplace of Joséphine, who later became Empress of France – is not exceptionally attractive. The splendors of the island are seen inland, in a mosaic of tropical forests and plantations, and along its beaches of black sand, under the threatening shadow of its capricious volcano, Montagne Pelée.

To the west, scattered in an incomparably blue sea and lulled by the trade winds, is

another British Crown colony. The British Virgin Islands are a micro-archipelago of more than fifty islands, including atolls, only part of them inhabited and all well worthy of their name. Perhaps in no other part of the Caribbean is nature so splendidly unspoiled. There are no high-rise hotel developments here, only peace and quiet amid secluded beaches lapped by translucent blue water

and the lushness of nature in the tropics. Virgin Gorda is the loveliest of the islands. It's a quiet backwater where there isn't even a proper town. It's little more than a succession of bays fringed with tall palm trees, against the vibrant green backdrop of a luxuriant forest. The Windward Islands – Dominica, St. Lucia, St. Vincent and Grenada – were also once British possessions, but they all gained their independence in the 1970s.

On these islands – perhaps because of their more southerly position – the mightiness and predominance of nature are evident at every turn. Amid the picture-postcard settings typical of the Caribbean, Dominica is a world apart. Its appeal does not lie in white beaches and breathtaking views of conventional tropical splendor. Here the beaches are formed of black, volcano-lava sand and the surface of the sea is often more than ruffled.

The harsher side of nature is revealed in places of outstanding beauty, especially inland, where impenetrable forests still cover much of the territory. For adventurous tourists who disdain the beach and its lazier pleasures, there is the excitement of exploring the Morne Trois Pitons National Park, in search of animals on the verge of extinction, or bathing in the freshwater springs dotted throughout the forest. The trails followed by tourists are those first trod by the Caribs centuries ago, and life on the island still proceeds at the leisurely pace of the old-world Caribbean.

As you stroll in the narrow streets of Roseau – the island's largest town, where tourists are still few and far between – its atmosphere exudes has an undeniable appeal. Much of the charm of Grenada too comes from its unspoiled natural environment. Amid the many extinct volcanoes at the heart of the island are sulfur lakes, rivers and sparkling waterfalls.

Although the island has relatively few beaches, unlike Dominica's they comply with the tropical norm. The loveliest beach is Grande Anse: a two-mile stretch of the finest sand, bordered by unbelievably transparent water. But what sets Grenada apart is the sweet, heady smell of spices that wafts through the air. The island's home produce – primarily nutmeg, but also saffron, vanilla, ginger, cinnamon and pepper – can be found on sale at the lively Saturday market in St. George's, the capital. It is a pretty town, once called the Portofino of the Caribbean, maybe on account of the red roofs of the handsome colonial dwellings set against the tropical green vegetation. Or maybe because St. George's lies on the gentle slopes of an extinct crater, the Carenage, which is a natural harbor and the best anchorage for miles around.

After conflict and violence in the recent past of Grenada, with intervention by United States marines in 1983, tourism is now expanding, but unhurriedly and with respect for the island's character: no sprawl of concrete and no buildings higher than the palm trees.

Sailing west we come to the Greater Antilles, larger islands whose past riches were the cause of the bloodiest battles. Here, people from Europe and Africa have mixed and mingled over the centuries to create a multiracial society, an exceptionally rich amalgam of different lands and influences. The contrasts and fusions are most striking in the largest islands.

The splendor of the colonialist era, when the Spanish ruled in cities such as Havana,

Trinidad and San Juan, is now gone and its remains are tinged with melancholy. It is sad to stroll down narrow streets of Havana Vieja at dusk and sense the presence of silent gardens, overwhelmed by tropical vegetation, behind the crumbling façades. Our mental wanderings are interrupted by the sound of music, emerging from the unexpected corners. Its cheerful notes, created with the richness of the African beat as its backdrop, banish our pensive mood. This irresistible music is perhaps the manifestation of the culture nurtured by whites and blacks, by Europe and Africa, and flourishing in the Caribbean.

As we explore the islands of the Caribbean – discovering their history, magic and mystery – the image of the vacationer's playground fades. Much more than an idyllic combination of sun, sea and sand, these islands embody the very essence of nature, its harsh realities as well as its warmth, as is surely fitting for a garden of Eden. And it is in this combination that the true charm and beauty of the Caribbean Islands lie.

A Taste of the Colonies

28 top *The modern harbor and Western-style public gardens are evidence of the British origins of Bridgetown, capital of Barbados.*

28 bottom *Sam Lord's Castle in Barbados was built in 1818 as a residence for the rich pirate.*

29 *Beyond the wrought-iron gate stands the imposing presidential palace of Santo Domingo.*

The fascination of Havana

30-31 *Stretching toward the ocean is the urban sprawl of Havana. With a population of over 2 million, it is one of the largest cities in Central America.*

31 top *Dominating one side of the immense Plaza de la Revolucion is the monument to José Martí, Cuban poet and national hero.*

31 center *When rich U.S. citizens fled the island after Fidel Castro's 1959 revolution, they left many cars behind. This one is a splendid and lovingly cared for Cadillac.*

31 bottom *In one of the most modern districts of Havana is the "City of Sport." Physical education and sporting traditions have an important place in Cuban life.*

32-33 *The Castillo de San Salvador de la Punta is one of the monumental fortresses built by the Spanish at the end of the 16th century to defend Havana and its bay.*

34-35 *With its neoclassical architecture, the imposing Capitolio Nacional, built in 1929, is clearly a copy of Washington, D.C.'s Capitol building.*

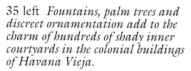

35 left *Fountains, palm trees and discreet ornamentation add to the charm of hundreds of shady inner courtyards in the colonial buildings of Havana Vieja.*

35 top right *The lovely square of the Parque Central is of 19th century origin. Pictured here behind the statue of José Martí, at the center of the rectangular square, is the delightful façade of the Hotel Inglaterra.*

35 center right *Presiding over Havana Vieja is an imposing military edifice, a reminder of the many wars and struggles that have colored the island's past.*

35 bottom right *Spanish taste and American colonial style have together produced the distinctive architecture of Havana's numerous monumental buildings.*

Trinidad and Santiago, pearls of central and southern Cuba

36 top *One of the cathedrals of Trinidad, a city rich in art and history; its magnificent old center is one of the best preserved in Latin America.*

36 bottom *Neoclassical architecture and pastel colors complement each other in the façade of this attractive building in Santiago de Cuba.*

36-37 *The Bahia di Santiago has one of the most sheltered harbors on the island of Cuba. It was from here that Conquistadors Cortez and Pizzarro set sail for South America.*

Santo Domingo, the oldest European settlement

38-39 *Built in 1510 by Viceroy Diego Colon, son of Christopher Columbus, the Alcazar de Colon is one of the most interesting remnants of Santo Domingo's former splendor.*

39 top *Inside the Alcazar is the richly decorated residence of the governor of Hispaniola. After the island's discovery, Santo Domingo continued to be its cultural and political center for a very long time.*

39 bottom *The Torre dello Homenaje – "the tower of tributes" – is part of the fortress located on the banks of the Rio Ozama.*

Enchanting cities of the Caribbean

40 top *Montego Bay is Jamaica's second biggest town. A lively and popular international tourist resort, it is also an important center of trade.*

40 bottom *The luxurious Club Gran Lido is one of the gems of Negril, a fashionable Jamaican resort that boasts almost 7 miles of beach.*

40-41 *Ocho Rios is a contemporary resort town, often visited for its excellent hotels and modern facilities.*

Traces of war in the heart of the tropics

43 top *The ruins of Fort Fleur d'Epée dominate the coast road close to Pointe des Chateaux in Guadeloupe.*

42 *At Fort-de-France in Martinique, the French flag flies from the bastions of Fort St. Louis. This magnificent fortress dates back to the 17th century.*

43 bottom *Built in the 1600s, Fort Frederik overlooks the small port of Frederiksted, which lies about 16 miles from Christiansted in St. Croix.*

44-45 *The war memorial of Pointe-à-Pitre in the center of Guadeloupe is surrounded by colonial buildings with elegant balconies.*

46-47 *On the island of St. Martin, the castle overlooking the town of Marigot offers a magnificent view of the bay. This island of the French Antilles is a much-sought-after anchorage for cruise liners. Its white-sand beaches, unspoiled coves and crystal-clear lagoons (as well as duty-free shopping) attract many tourists.*

St. Pierre,
the Caribbean's own Pompei

48-49 *St. Pierre, the small port of Martinique, is known as the Pompeii of the Caribbean: the town was completely destroyed in 1902 by a violent eruption of Montagne Pelée, which looms menacingly over it.*

50-51 *Vessels of every kind - from sailing boats to luxury cruise ships - moor in the busy port of Charlotte Amalie in the Virgin Islands.*

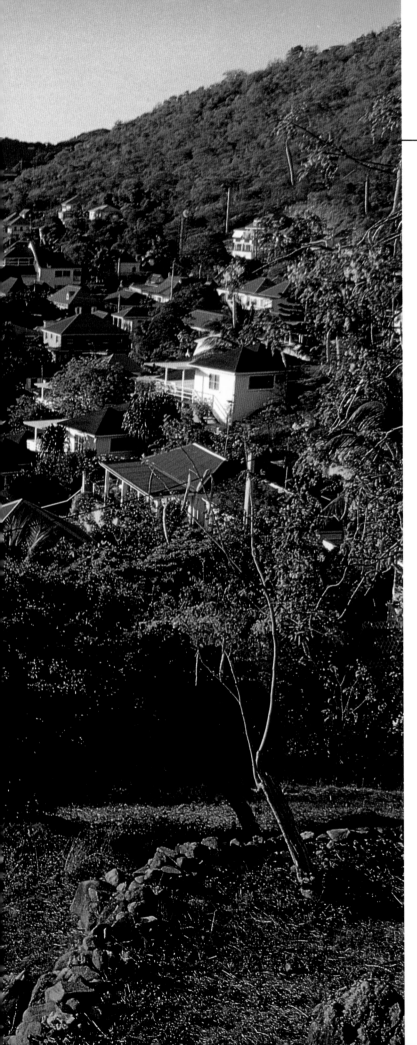

Tropical sun,
à la francaise

52-53 *The red roofs of Gustavia are a reminder of France's role in the settlement of St. Barthélemy. The town has a well-sheltered natural harbor, which is often visited by luxury yachts.*

From Ebony to Ivory

54 top *Waiting on the jetty to greet tourists arriving in Grenada is a carnival-style parade; dominating the scene are the vibrant colors typical of the Caribbean.*

54 bottom *The market at Pointe-à-Pitre dominates the harbor area, stretching along jetties where locals buy the daily catch straight from the fishing boats.*

55 *The huge Saturday market brings a crowd to St. George's, capital city of Grenada. People often buy the home-grown spices for which the island is famous.*

Music and high spirits to the tempo of the Tropics

56 *Any time of day is right for
music and dancing.*

57 *Straw hats and brightly
colored shirts create a picturesque
islander.*

58-59 *There is natural beauty
everywhere in the Tropics.*

Martinique and Guadeloupe: sun, sea and ... Creole culture

60-61 *Martinique and Guadeloupe are citadels of the Creole language and culture. And there still exists a strong link between Africa and the islands of the Caribbean.*

62-63 *The colorful market in Basse-Terre, second-largest town of Guadeloupe, offers a splendid assortment of island produce - fruit, vegetables, spices and flour.*

64-65 *Along these volcanic beaches of gray sand, traditional fishing methods are still used today.*

66-67 *Located at the eastern tip of Guadeloupe, St. François is considered the St. Tropez of the Caribbean.*

68-69 *As evening draws on, a group of fishermen linger on the beach that borders the Malecón in Havana.*

69 top *A fire-eater entertaining in Calle Obispo in Habana Vieja, a street of rebuilt houses painted in the traditional pastel colors.*

69 center and bottom *More than two-thirds of the people of Cuba have a Caribbean heritage mingled with African and European influences.*

70 top and center *Cayo Coco is the largest of the islands in the archipelago off the coast of Ciego de Avila. It is a paradise of clear water, white sand and sun. Low palms fringe the beaches where every kind of sport is practiced.*

70 bottom *The islands of the archipelago are uninhabited, with the exceptions of Cayo Coco and Cayo Giullermo where tourist facilities have been built. Their effects on the natural environment are monitored by scientists from Havana University.*

71 *The passion for golf, imported from Britain and America, has led to the development of some amazing golf courses clinging to rocky clifftops.*

Barbados, shades of Little England

72-73 In Bridgetown, capital
of Barbados, Independence Day
is celebrated with a traditional
parade that has
plenty of Caribbean charm.
A British colony since 1625, the
island became independent in
1966; it is now a member of the
British Commonwealth.

74 *A few miles from the capital of Barbados is Oistins, the town where the "Barbados Charter" establishing British rule was signed in 1625. The locals of Oistins pictured here are attending Sunday service.*

75 *Churchgoers display Western dress as well as indigenous attire. In the graveyard adjoining Oistins church is a crypt called "Mystery Vault," said to be haunted by ghosts.*

Island with an African heart

76-77 *African culture is very much alive in the "melting pot" culture of the Caribbean.*

78-79 *The flamboyant carnival held in Grenada, southernmost of the Windward Islands, owes much to Creole folklore, a mixture of European and African religious beliefs.*

Earth's Last Eden

80 top *Swept by the trade winds, La Vache bay is one of the most beautiful spots on the island of Trinidad.*

80 bottom *At some distance from Guadeloupe, facing the promontory of Pointe des Chateaux, the tiny islands of Petite-Terre offer unspoiled nature.*

81 *With white sand and deep-blue ocean fringed by tall palms and the coral reef just offshore, the beach of Las Cuevas Bay in Trinidad may reflect your idea of paradise.*

The heavenly beaches of paradise on Earth

82 top Wind-bent palm trees overhang one of the delightful beaches south of Punta Cana, in the vicinity of the Bavaro Hotel in Santo Domingo in the Dominican Republic.

82 bottom Facing Isla Saona in Santo Domingo is the shady beach of Ventaglio Club Dominicus resort hotel.

83 *The rainbow colors of sailing boats moored at Punta Cana, a smart resort close to Santo Domingo, are reflected in the turquoise waters.*

84-85 *Set in the deep blue of the Caribbean is the small Isla Saona, an unspoiled island just off the southern shores of the Dominican Republic.*

86-87 *The splendor of Jamaica's northern coast is revealed in this picture taken near Port Antonio, a small town with a magnificent and well-sheltered double harbor.*

88 top *The countryside inland from Ocho Rios, a popular resort town, has some of the loveliest scenery in Jamaica. Trekking on horseback is an ideal way to explore.*

88 bottom *With pools of blue-green water rimmed with rocks and greenery, the cliffs of Negril are one of Jamaica's foremost tourist attractions.*

89 *The lush vegetation in Jamaica appears to lay siege to the tiny bay of Navy Island, just off Port Antonio.*

90-91 *Cays are small low islets of coral sand, typically found in the tropical seas of the Caribbean. Around the coast of Cuba there are more than 350.*

91 top *Coral beaches, crystal-clear waters and seabeds teeming with life: Cayo Largo epitomizes the natural splendor of the Caribbean.*

91 center and bottom *Cayo Largo is a stunning stretch of sand, 19 miles long and 7 miles wide. With its dazzling colors and enormous variety of underwater flora and fauna, it rivals even the most celebrated coral reefs.*

92 top *The picturesque bays of St. Barthélemy are frequented by affluent tourists; the secluded setting and crystal-clear water of Anses de Lorient makes it one of the most popular on the island.*

92 bottom *The short runway of St. Barthélemy's tiny airport has not spoiled the enchanting picture presented by Anse de St. Jean, with its unbelievably blue sea.*

93 *Possibly the longest and most famous beach of St. Barthélemy is Anse des Flamands, a never-crowded strip of fine-grain sand, sheltered from wind and breakers.*

94-95 *Anses de Lorient is surely one of St. Barthélemy's loveliest beaches. St. Bart's, as the island is called by the locals, was first settled by the French and then leased to the Swedes in 1785 for about a century. Breton and Norman dialects are still spoken in a few of its villages, a reminder of the island's past.*

96-97 *Anse des Flamands is considered one of the most beautiful beaches in the world. Its protected position ensures that this long stretch of fine white sand is never troubled by the winds and occasional storms that sweep across the island of St. Barthélemy.*

The islands of the capricious giant

Crystal-clear waters

100-101 *Lapped by the blue-green ocean, the beach and bay of Marigot are the foremost attractions of the capital town of St. Martin's French half. Major contributions to the scene are made by Fort St. Louis, with its panorama of the bay, and the tourist marina that attracts hundreds of fine boats.*

102-103 *Off the southern coast of Cuba is Cayo Largo (in Spanish its name sounds like "long street"), a 90-kilometer strip of white coral sand.*

104-105 *Brown-sand beaches and gently rolling hills thick with vegetation are typical features of the coastline of Basse-Terre and unmistakable evidence of the island's volcanic origin.*

106-107 *La Pointe des Chateaux is a long tongue of land extending from the island of Grande-Terre toward the Atlantic and terminating in wind-swept cliffs.*

110-111 *The terrain in Guadeloupe's interior is generally covered with vegetation. Dense tropical forests grow in the valleys and on the mountains, the mass of green occasionally interrupted by the rushing water that forces its way through the undergrowth.*

Guadeloupe, the call of the rainforest

108 *High up in the heart of the Parc Naturel de Guadeloupe, columns of steam rise from the volcanic vents of Soufrière.*

109 *In the Parc Naturel de Guadeloupe, the Chutes du Carbet are an impressive sight, plunging down through the vegetation of the tropical rainforest.*

The Virgin Islands, wonders of the Caribbean

112 and 113 top *Renowned for its unspoiled beauty, the island of St. John is practically undeveloped and undisturbed. Much of its territory is part of the Virgin Islands National Park.*

113 bottom *A catamaran has beached on the smooth sand of Buck Island, one of the gems of the U.S. Virgin Islands.*

114-115 *This enchanting place is Trunk Bay on St. John, the most virgin of the U.S. Virgin Islands. It is generally considered the loveliest beach on St. John, favored by scuba enthusiasts as a departure point for stunning dives.*

St. Lucia,
home of the twin volcanoes

116-117 *On the west coast of St. Lucia, where it's rivaled only by Castries and Rodney Bay, Marigot Bay is one of the most fascinating bays of the Caribbean. Its small but well-equipped harbor is busy with boats year-round.*

118-119 *Prominent against the horizon are the green peaks of the twin volcanoes Gros Piton and Petit Piton. Soaring from the sea to a height of 2,300 feet, their shapely forms are a distinctive landmark on St. Lucia.*

Land of corals

120 *The hundred or so islands and cays that make up the archipelago of the Grenadines, scattered between Grenada and St. Vincent, offer an idyllic setting for sailing and underwater fishing.*

121 *Every shade of blue and green is blended in the warm waters around the tiny island of Petit Tabac in the Grenadines.*

122 *The underwater world of the Tropics holds constant surprises for divers, like this encounter with an angelfish.*

123 top *Many kinds of life-forms exist on the floor of the Caribbean Sea, where breeding and growth are encouraged by favorable currents. This type and size of sponge is often seen in these waters.*

123 bottom *For some creatures, living on a tropical coral reef can mean a constant struggle to survive. Here a branching sponge fights for living space with two "bushes" of fire-red coral.*

124 top *A colony of deep-red corals has taken root on the wall of a reef. For scuba divers there are many stunning sights in the Caribbean.*

124 bottom *Long-snouted dolphins* (Stenidae) *are among the most playful of all sea mammals. In the waters of the Caribbean it isn't unusual to come across these gregarious creatures swimming alone or in groups. In either case they appear to enjoy the company of divers.*

125 *Spotted and blue-striped fish in search of food swim close to a huge coral fan. The bright Caribbean light and the shallow water around many of the coral reefs make visibility below the surface excellent, and divers can take splendid photos.*

126-127 *St. John, one of the U.S. Virgin Islands, has been described as "an unspoiled tropical paradise." Its reputation is borne out by its sparse population (only 3,000 people), a national park (since 1956) occupying practically the entire island, and assorted coves, inlets and beaches where pristine nature can still be found.*

128 *The colors of the setting sun light up Dickenson Bay, one of the "365 beaches" that the islanders of Antigua love to lay claim to. This bay vies with Runway Bay as the resort offering the finest tourist amenities on all Antigua.*